A THIN LINE BETWEEN LOVE & HATE

KELLEY Y. SCHOOLS
2016

ISBN-13:978-0692455340 (KELLEY SCHOOLS)
ISBN-10: 0692455345
APRIL 2016

COPYRIGHT 2016 KELLEY SCHOOLS
LIBRARY OF CONGRESS COPYRIGHT PUBLICATION
SCHOOLS, KELLEY

ALL RIGHTS RESERVED, INCLUDING THE RIGHT TO REPRODUCE THIS BOOK OR PORTIONS THEREOF IN ANY FORM WHATSOEVER.

MANUFACTURED IN THE UNITED STATES

CONTACT KELLEY:
WWW.KELLY_SCHOOLS@HOTMAIL.COM
WWW.KELLEYSCHOOLS.COM

ACKNOWLEDGEMENTS

First and foremost, I thank God for giving me a gift that I can share with the rest of the world. This is my fifth poetry book I can remember thinking in the beginning where do I go from here and now I know the sky is the limit and I will keep soaring for as long and as high as I can until I reach my desired destination. I thank my parents for raising me to be an independent woman, encouraging me to take chances in life and to be as happy as I can be taking nothing for granted and living life to the fullest. I am thankful for my children, my family and friends that continue to support me in all of my endeavors where would I be without you. Thank you for allowing me to share my world with yours as I continue to dance like no one is watching....

TABLE OF CONTENTS

LOVE
- Indescribable
- Deep Thought
- Illusion
- I Am Sure
- Love
- Feelings
- Connection
- Unbreakable
- When my wants become my needs
- Lovers and Friends

HATE
- Release My Soul
- Broken Heart
- The Struggle
- A Thin Line Between Love & Hate
- Still I Shine
- Inconsistencies
- I see the light
- Confusion
- Tainted Love

LOVE

INDESCRIBABLE

The Electricity that flows through my veins when we make love drives me insane. The love we share will always remain.

The essence of our very souls collide into a stream of pure unadulterated bliss and the heartfelt feeling with each and every kiss that brings you to the point of no return it's you that my heart yearns.

That indescribable feeling, I get as you rise between my thighs keeps me on the most ultimate high. The intimacy is off the chain in ways I couldn't imagine just shook for real off the break mmmmn and the way my legs shake ain't nothing better than making love to my number one go getter.

The way you caress and awaken the very existence of my being not only shows me but I can truly feel the meaning....

DEEP THOUGHT

Thinking about you so much that it woke me up out of the deepest sleep it was so real I thought it was for keeps.

It was completely off the hook I had to reflect back to see if I called out your name I was completely shook.

The remnants of you they still remain and the love that I have in my heart drives me totally insane.

Anxiety has taken hold of me I'm trying not to be so bold but you know me and you know my heart some things will never ever part especially not the feeling I have for you in my heart......

ILLUSION

I can't explain what you do to me my thoughts of you caress me mentally.

I am so intrigued with you that I can't contain my feelings there's that connection that just keeps reeling me in.

I close my eyes and shutter at the thought of more to come to just begin, to be an actual reality.

You are breath of fresh air, a cleansing of the soul our connection is sooo deep I am completely losing control the attraction is so unreal even without touching I can feel.

I AM SURE

As each day goes by
     I am missing you more and more
But there is a calmness, a calmness
     In my soul that tells me
I am sure.......

I am sure, sure of myself and
     Sure of my relationship with you
I cannot predict the span of time
     But what I do know
Is that I want your body, soul and mind....

LOVE

No matter how many times I look into your eyes
I see the realization that love truly resides.

It surfaces in your eyes from the very existence of
your soul.
I can feel it without touching, talking without
speaking as our hearts dance to the beat of just one
drum.

A drum that beats so loud yet carries a tune so
profound that it lingers in the depths of my entire
being long after the music has gone I can sway to the
beat as the rhythm flows on.......

FEELINGS

The feeling of closeness that I get when I'm with you cannot be compared to any other I can close my eyes and feel your touch damn I've missed you much no need to cover the truth of lovers.

I was speechless held bound by feelings that I can't deny all I could do was close my eyes and sigh. Thoughts of making love to you consumed me all night I just couldn't get right.

Thoughts of wanting to no hell needing to feel you sent a sensation so strong that I couldn't sit still just thinking about it for too long....

CONNECTION

From the first moment we formally introduced ourselves instantly the mental and the physical connection was there, a simultaneous bond seemed to form and interests and information was shared I was very much like damn he could get it he could be my man.

I always knew that you existed as you I but up until this point our lives we never shared a conversation let alone share a few laughs but I find myself thinking I should have taken another path along the way; all the bells going off in my head keeping ringing your name.

As thoughts of you constantly running through my mind driving me crazy, the possibilities are endless under all these pretenses that I am feeling this from the depths of my soul. I am trying to get a grip but it's like my inner soul cries out to you and my inner being has taken hold. The hold is unbelievably surreal these feelings are so strong I can actually feel.

My thoughts and feelings I have profoundly expressed to you I may be a little over bearing at times but you confessed you feel it to. All I know is that my innermost thoughts are daring me to reach out to you, to claim you to claim us and it will become true and the thoughts of having a future together as one with you...

UNBREAKABLE

I keep playing this scene in my mind every time I close my eyes thoughts of you right between my thighs sends a bolt of electricity with a force so strong that in my heart love for you will forever belong.

The thought of you touching me in places I could only dream of has now surfaced and are ready to be unleashed and embellished as we make love, make memories to share way beyond compare of a love with another that I have never shared.

Looking into your eyes has always made me realize that this love regardless of the level, regardless of other relationships is truly real. The bond is unbreakable the complexity is out of this world and I know without a shadow of a doubt I'm always going to be that girl....

WHEN MY WANTS BECOME NEEDS

Meeting of the minds to me the most physical attraction that feeds into what you actually want in a relationship. I want to take my time to get to know you your mental speaks volumes to my heart the most sacred part. I need to feel that mental connection which makes the love true, knowing you inside and out and when we make love our bodies will scream and shout.

Shouting in a wave of ecstasy the connection is that strong and there will be no doubt in where you belong. Good friends make the best lovers and will lead to unforgettable forever's that we are searching for I know I want you I know I need more. I want no I need my best friend to be there when I need you and you being there for me, a lifetime of lovers and best friends together to grow old and the love never ends.

Our circle will be complete and anyone else we come in contact with is automatic defeat because I know in my heart you are the one for me this is not just a want it is a need and I know we can succeed.

There is no one else that I feel is more equal to me than you and you have expressed your feelings to me to. I want to progress with you, make a future with you and never let you go. I need to feel you our mental conversations fill me with so much joy and I know I do that for you come on boy let's make this a love story come true...

LOVERS AND FRIENDS

Thinking of the way you caress me when we make love, the way you take your time as we make love with our bodies and our minds.

You give me all of you as I give myself this connection is embedded in our souls and I can feel it flow through my body even in the tips of my toes.

Making love to you leaves me with an ultimate high never wanting to say bye but knowing we will be in each other's arms again soon my lover my friend.

HATE

RELEASE MY SOUL

Please release my soul in which I've allowed you too much control when I decided to let love grab hold of me and now I've lost something near and dear to me...

I've allowed you to consume me to the point that I don't even recognize who I am. Damn .... I'm not sure when all this took place but it's time to erase all traces of you in order to save me then that's what I have to do.

Please release my soul in which I've allowed you too much control when I decided to let love grab a hold of me and now I've lost something near and dear to me...

I always put you first, your needs before mine you're wants no matter what kind is a travesty of sorts, it's time for you to find another port. I've allowed you to rent this space for too long as if this is where you belong, this tune is played out it's time for another song.

You have now taken complete advantage of the situation with no anticipation that one day I would come to the realization and walk the other way it's time to let go and say....

Please release my soul in which I've allowed you too much control when I've decided to let love grab hold of me and now I've lost something near and dear to me that I have to get back......myself

BROKEN HEART

How do you live with a broken heart that has been lied to, beaten and bruised, and broken into a million pieces but yet you choose to stay; telling yourself that he will change and that everything will be okay. All the while deep in your heart you know the best thing for you to do is part and pick up the remaining pieces of your heart and walk away.

Walk away knowing that you kept it 100, you provided the experience that he feeds from, that he draws energy and lives off of but he can't replenish that charge without your expertise, and your mind keeps telling your heart to let go, to just release.

Release those feelings past and move on at last you have done all that you could to build a life with this man and in reality he doesn't do all he can, he has gotten comfortable even though you're not and even though you have expressed your feelings he's not.

Not being honest, not being fair even though he can see you're at your wits end and pulling out your hair;

It still doesn't compare to what you have done for him and the benefits are real though it's through your hard work and sweat and he just doesn't care on money you can bet. It is time to raise the bar if you will get your plan together and put it in motion to sit him still, and even though he doesn't get it he will and when you say it's over you just keeping it real....

After all he already knows the deal he just continues to carry on until you get fed up and all hope is gone and then he will be forced to gather his things and by this time friendship is a thing of the past, hatred has stepped in and removed any ounce of love that was left but as you have already stated it is the end where time waits for no one time for you to live without him....

THE STRUGGLE

You think I will always be here to secure your current and your future but that is a cut that will soon require a suture. I can't keep living a lie that only benefits you because everything that I am experiencing for me just ain't true. No feelings of love in my mind just the thoughts of biding time until I am free of all things without understanding no need to keep talking or feel like reprimanding.

I can no longer sit by and watch you take advantage of me time and time again this is not what lovers do hell it ain't even for friends. So you see I need to take control of my life and do what I need to do for me, this life we living ain't real so what is the point on trying to seal this deal.

You sit back while I push myself and struggle to have a better life to make a way and everything is cool as long as you have a place to stay, you cannot step up to the plate because hard work and the struggle is something in which you can't even relate.

Instead of me being overjoyed with love I'm being consumed with thoughts of hate I can't keep allowing the devil to spoil the food that's on my plate...

I have tolerated this enough and it is time to move forward and have the life that I have always wanted and clearly an indication that involves you has gone out the window with all of your broken promises and lies that you don't intend to do just trying to make a way for yourself and only worried about you. Selfishness does not become you but it will in time make a better me and in time you will see......

A THIN LINE BETWEEN LOVE & HATE

The feeling you get in the pit of your stomach when you realize the man you have been in a relationship over a period of years doesn't love you the way you love him. The love you thought you shared has no equality, the value has deprecated tremendously over time. There is no benefit when you think about it at least to you when you list pros and cons as a means to decide from this point what you need to do. Where do we go from here?

There is definitely a difference between loving someone and being in love with someone yes it's true for your own sanity you need to pick up the pieces and do what's best for you. When someone shows you who they are the first time please believe them, you cannot think that someone is going to change because in reality all they do is rearrange things to appear to be a certain way and as we know all things that happen in the dark will always surface to light and then things twist and turn into a different plight.

The realization of life and how you are living smacks you dead in the face.

You decide to have the dreaded talk to confirm the things you already know to be true and once you hear the truth even then he doesn't admit the voice of reason confirms it all there is nothing left to do as the tears slowly fall you realize that it's not your loss even though it feels like it but in fact he know it's his. You have tried to reason with him to work things out but how can he contribute if he acts like he doesn't know what you are talking about. He has decided to go the road less traveled and as long as that works for him don't you dare become unraveled.

Stay focused men live for the day woman plan on what steps they need to take to get them where they need to be and by the time its' too late he will eventually see that you were the woman that held him down but what goes around comes back around and before long it all will be a thing of the past....

STILL I SHINE

Nobody knows what I go through day in and day out inside these walls of mine not my struggle, the highs, my lowest points but I still shine.

Shine like a diamond you will never see me succumb to defeat of any kind that shit only happens to a weak mind I ain't got time. You can try to put yourself in my shoes and say what you would do but you can't rock like me that I know that to be true.

Faced with adversary time and time again can't keep a good girl down even if I ended up with a clown. Let the show begin I'll always come out on top in the end. No matter how hard you come at me and try to break me my faith is too strong and despite your devilish ways. I've realized with you I don't belong.

Never did but it took me sometime to accept it for what it really is and the truth is you ain't mine we just living on borrowed time....

I am looking for something at this point in my life I'm not sure if I'll ever find a love for me that will be all mine.

Never been a wanderer I always give my all but it always seems as if I am built up to take a fall. When I love, I love hard no median to partake but then as time goes on as always out comes his past mistakes.

I want a love that will love me back in return of what I'm giving not just to stand idle without really giving or living.

From the outside looking in I'm as happy as can be but deep down inside there is no one loving me as I need the love to be. I have sacrificed all that I am willing to do for causes that don't bring me gratification too. I've realized that true love hasn't found me yet only pieces some of love and some of regret that I've managed to get. Pieces that don't amount to the real thing just particles strong enough to remain and now in my heart I know that the two are not the same......

INCONSISTENCIES

The inconsistencies remain even though at this point in my life it doesn't drive me insane. I have gathered my thoughts and got my mind in the right frame. You are going to do you regardless no matter what you even seem heartless at times but me I am always going to be me and there is more that is coming you will see.

You will see that my life doesn't revolve around you and just because I don't question things doesn't mean I believe them to be true but I'm going to do me and you going to do you.

I have relished in the truth saw the light if you will no need to aim if I don't plan to shoot and kill actions speak louder than words I just need to show you the deal. I can move forward without you there is nothing left to hold onto time after time you have succeeded in showing me your worth and what cards you display and I continue to sashay as if things are good and then you fall back as I knew you would.

I am embarking on a new me if you weren't too busy with yourself and what you do would clearly see that life goes on and I am redefining me. Living for me and all that will make me happy even if it means leaving you well hell in my mind at this point you are already gone.......

I SEE THE LIGHT

Darkness doesn't become me and I can't allow it to consume me. The darkness I feel when I'm alone the funny part of it all is that you could be sitting right next to me and nothing changes; it is time for things to be rearranged. I don't need a man to validate me especially one that can barely compliment me it's not about the exterior though your life is based on an illusion as in the way you sell yourself. I have finally come to the conclusion that this thing right here doesn't really fit into what I actually need and more so where I am going the ironic part is your living your life not knowing.

You think that you have everyone fooled in a sense but every time I think about it I wince at the thought that you are definitely not who I thought you were, and when I look back there were plenty of signs but the only thing that registered for me was that I wanted you to be mine.

Sometimes I wish you would just walk right out the door. I do believe that you are blocking my blessings and when you are gone there will be more.

More doors will open, more choices to this life I am living because I just don't think of myself I am always giving. Giving for the common good of mankind, giving for a love that I want to be able to call all mine.

I am always contributing to love and happiness that if I give it will come until I had to face the reality that I am not sure if I will ever be the only one. Life is too short to be unhappy and lose sight of the very thing I am trying to hold onto myself, love and happiness I want and deserve more....

CONFUSION

I am not sure which way to go the stats are posted it's not like I don't know but I am confused. Confused because I love you in so many ways but I also know you are not good for me and it is going to continue to cost me if you stay.

It's like my soul cries out to you when you leave and when you're here I am forced to accept the realization that I am being deceived. The late night calls and texts that you don't think I recognize the pattern but I don't need a lantern I just don't speak on it there is no need to I just have to do what I have to do.

The constant reminders of past mistakes that I thought I could shake keep popping up and forcing me to relate the two and the more I try to drown it out it keeps surfacing and I can see it every time I look at you. No doubt my love is real but at this point in my life I don't see any point in sealing any deals I just need time to work things through, time to help myself get over you.

This is really hard to do spending almost a decade of time with a man that at least fifty percent of the time wasn't really true. These actions have hardened my heart in ways that I never really knew until I starting comparing other people to you. I want to be able to walk away and not take the pain with me. I want the next man to truly see me for who I am and not what I have been through; I want him to see that with me love can really be true.

Even though I have felt unbearable pain at times I have made it through there is no way in hell I will let you win that just wouldn't do. I have accepted this situation for exactly what it is as well as accepting the part that I played the blame cannot be so easily laid on you I knew the deal and I know you....

TAINTED LOVE

This right here is plain stupidity this thing we call love has no validity it is as phony as a three dollar bill I can't believe after all this time why in the same place I remain still. It is not like you have the wool pulled over my eyes at this point there is nothing else that could surprise me about you, this ain't the life for me and your love will never be true.

Tainted on all levels everything is all disheveled a plain old catastrophe that was never meant to be only the acceptance of the love that was never there for me. How dare you continue to play this game of charades in more ways than one, the only difference is that my time has come. The time has come to remove myself from this situation even though there is so much contemplation on my part, the things we do to ease the pain of a broken heart.

Broken hearts do mend its true but I guess you never thought that I would give up you know its true. Old habits are so bad to break but this aint your first rodeo so I know you can relate. Relate to the fact that here you are once again a hand full of lovers but no real friends the cycle of life as you see it once again has come to an end.

A blind man could see that this is the end don't worry no need to see about me. I am embarking on a plateau of many where life will be fabulous and love will be plenty. I made this bed and lie in it a little longer I will but the difference is I am moving on and that's real....

Check out other books by this Author

www.ingramcontent.com/pod-product-compliance
Lightning Source LLC
Chambersburg PA
CBHW051713090426
42736CB00013B/2688